Short Stories

Frida Braide

BookLeaf Publishing

India | USA | UK

Presentation by *BookLeaf Publishing*

Web: www.bookleafpub.com

E-mail: info@bookleafpub.com

ISBN: 9789358319101

First edition 2023

ONE

boundless world around
hidden secrets
with a restless sky
expanse of gray
extraordinary dense
warm sensation
oak
sprightly whispered mischief
hidden   warm vibration
imagination
interior
wondrous world
clouds gathered air cold
golden strange
keepers

TWO

alleyway bustling
eyes
vibrant fade
breath air
gnawing feeling
echoed   shadowy
deepest void
corner space
glimpse unknown
guardians   fade
souls mark tirelessly
focus stone
brush spot

THREE

wild
Gray clouds   howled
advancing forsaken   twen- ty—
resilience alongside
ocean firm
emptiness forgotten
lying   frayed   faded
defeated humble tired
powerful

FOUR

untamed
fire   revelation
ethereal anticipation
realm
profound   revealed
aching wisdom
complexities anticipation
truths deeper
desire   darkness
merely doubts
dreams insecurities
mingled   uncertain   rawness

FIVE

forgotten dusty experiences
yellow darkness
wordless
unravel intertwined
forsaken
overexposed alive
shadows   lost
remnants   present

SIX

nestled significance
blue
expose dreamscape
embrace
stretched air
fragments
ponder beyond night
despite nothingness
ordinary
forever
fleeting eternal
courage
wonders
emerged perception

SEVEN

heart weathered
presens guarding sanctuary
echoes
snake wings held by
divine stones
existence promised bound
worn death glory
duality confined
infinite embrace
ruins faded found
watchful

EIGHT

redemption
starts overlooked
sought consumed
muffled understanding
dreams relentless
distanced voices
fulfillment circular
pursuit of resonance genuine

NINE

structure complex
sounds patterns clues
together
simmering revealing
alien earth being dormant
potential sparked
the accidental vastness
humbling the echoes

TEN

crisp
stone jewels
rock raindrops
wind diamonds
tranformation
sculptures
moment
sculpture passing ice
eternal

ELEVEN

isolated trivial breath
passages
deteriorated holding
beyond knowledge of desperation
serendipitous
unwavering old
hope humbling
rebuilding determination
between

TWELVE

shoulders hearts
Relics
soaring T
ruins oblivion
act forgotten
escape home
spectacle performing despair
sadness flourished
forged obliterated
resilience fallen

THIRTHEEN

facade
tainted collapse
deception unspoken hidden
seemingly lie
embracing fulfilled
controlled compassion chaos
symbol emerged imperfection
conformity

FOURTHEEN

figure
blended shadow
intertwined
cherishing obscured emotion
watching yearning
motionless enveloped possibilities

FIFTHEEN

15

exposed bore
aftermath glimmer
flood destruction wellspring learning
echoes realized
perspective extinguish within

SIXTHEEN

vast depths
phantoms teased
concealed tides
introspection boundless
labyrint panterns morphing
sky shapes hiding
found essence

SEVENTHEEN

realm breeze
tomorrow
reflection
sands taught fragments
revealed knowledge ebbs
guding scattered experiences
memory dissolved

EIGHTEEN

paused messy landscape
plastic
passerby mundande mirrored
tall form
gentle urban
firmly serious play

NINETHEEN

quaint remarkable transformation
petals replicate enchanting
reveal secrets
dipped unfolded
breath honor
sacred
miraculous faded
singular
wondrous water
gasps applause
copy transition
backdrop indistinguishable form
witness
resplendent
enduring cycle

TWENTY

remote waves twist
growing desolation
horizon outside
harsh treacherous metal
purpose vessel spotted
representation surface
visitor forsaken red
quiet connection
power temporary forged

TWENTYONE

heart chaos flowers
brisk amidst
palpable within
strained tornado
importance symbolized
exchanges overshadowed
overwhelming crack reduced
fiercest storms
uprooted metaphor